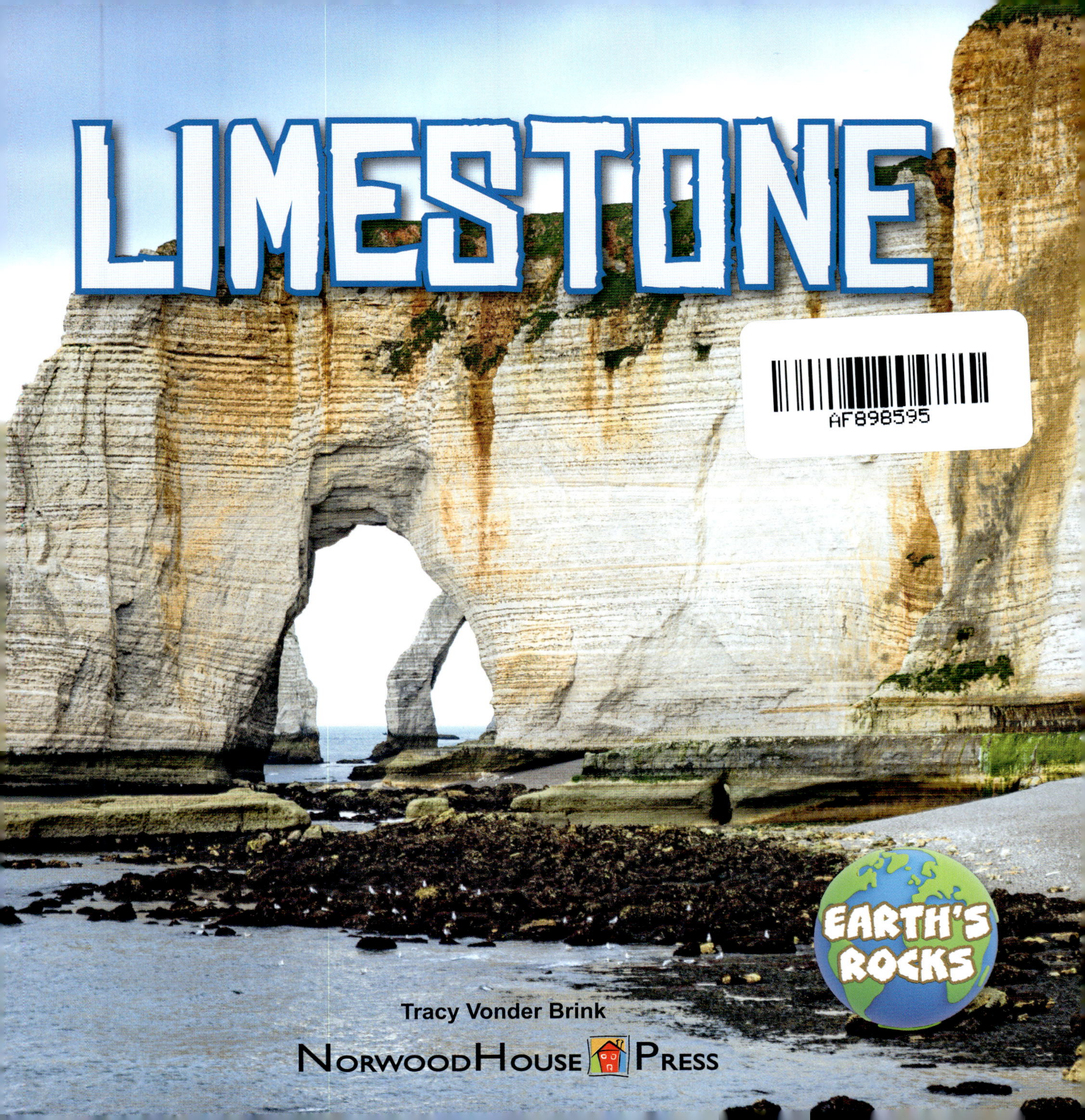

LIMESTONE

EARTH'S ROCKS

Tracy Vonder Brink

NorwoodHouse Press

Cataloging-in-Publication Data

Names: Vonder Brink, Tracy.
Title: Limestone / Tracy Vonder Brink.
Description: Buffalo, NY : Norwood House Press, 2027. | Series: Earth's rocks | Includes glossary and index.
Identifiers: ISBN 9781978580084 (pbk.) | ISBN 9781978580091 (library bound) | ISBN 9781978580107 (ebook)
Subjects: LCSH: Limestone--Juvenile literature. | Sedimentary rocks--Juvenile literature.
Classification: LCC QE471.V66 2027 | DDC 552.5--dc23

Published in 2027 by
Norwood House Press
2544 Clinton Street
Buffalo, NY 14224

Designer: Rhea Magaro
Editor: Kim Thompson

Photo credits: Cover, p. 1 Chris WM Willemsen/Shutterstock.com; p. 3 Parmna/Shutterstock.com; p. 4 Kavic.C/Shutterstock.com; p. 5 Kira_G/Shutterstock.com; p. 6 Yes058 Montree Nanta/Shutterstock.com; p. 7 vveronka/Shutterstock.com; p. 8 BlueRingMedia/Shutterstock.com; p. 9 Iwan Hainim/Shutterstock.com; p. 11 Vladislav Gajic/Shutterstock.com; p. 12 AHua69/Shutterstock.com; p. 13 Luc V. de Zeeuw/Shutterstock.com; p. 14 Wikipedia; p. 15 Dennis MacDonald/Shutterstock.com; p. 17 Cole Kujawa/Shutterstock.com; p. 18 bogubogu/Shutterstock.com; p. 19 Shanjaya/Shutterstock.com; p. 21 wavebreakmedia/Shutterstock.com;

Printed in the United States of America

CPSIA compliance information: Batch #CSNHP27: For further information contact Norwood House Press at 1-800-237-9932.

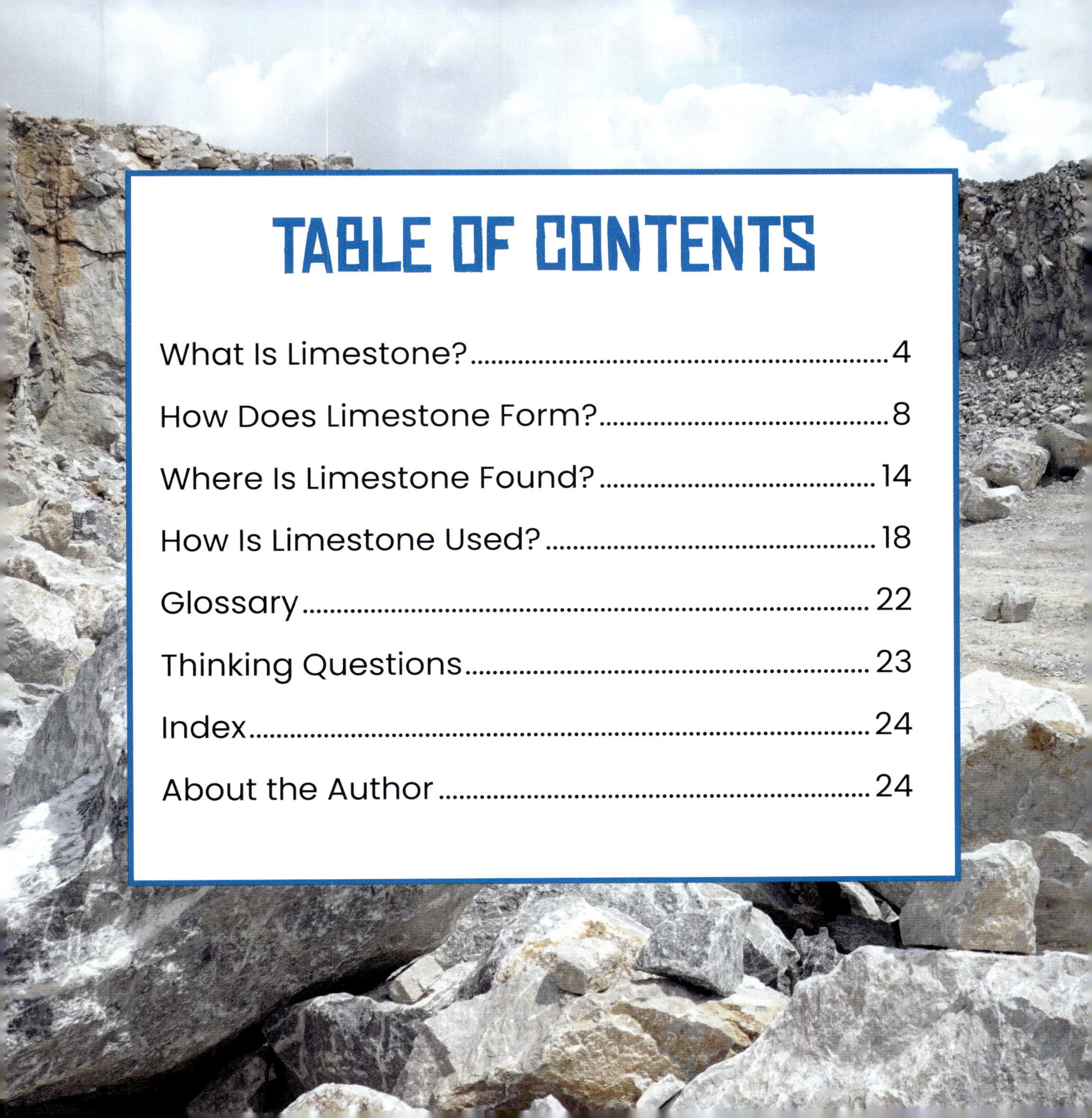

TABLE OF CONTENTS

WHAT IS LIMESTONE?

Rocks make up many things in the world, from tall mountains to the deep seafloor. All rocks are made of **minerals**. They are put into three main groups based on how they form.

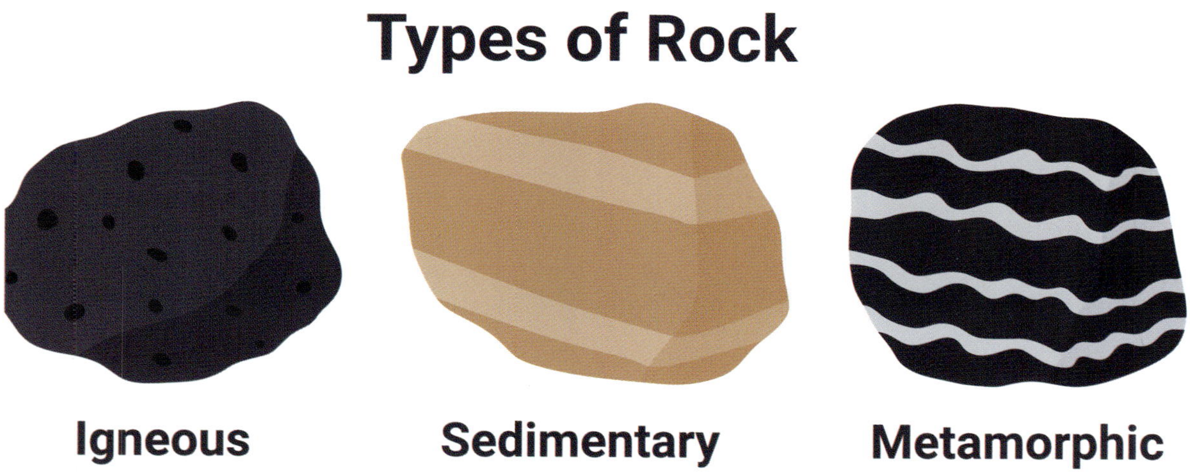

Some sedimentary rocks start out as bits of long-dead animals. Limestone is this kind of sedimentary rock.

Most limestone comes from the **fossils** of sea animals. Sometimes you can see the fossils in the rock, but not always. A mineral found in the fossils makes limestone fizz when **vinegar** is poured on it!

Limestone is often white, gray, or light brown.

Some can be yellow or even pink.

HOW DOES LIMESTONE FORM?

Like all rocks, limestone forms during Earth's rock cycle.

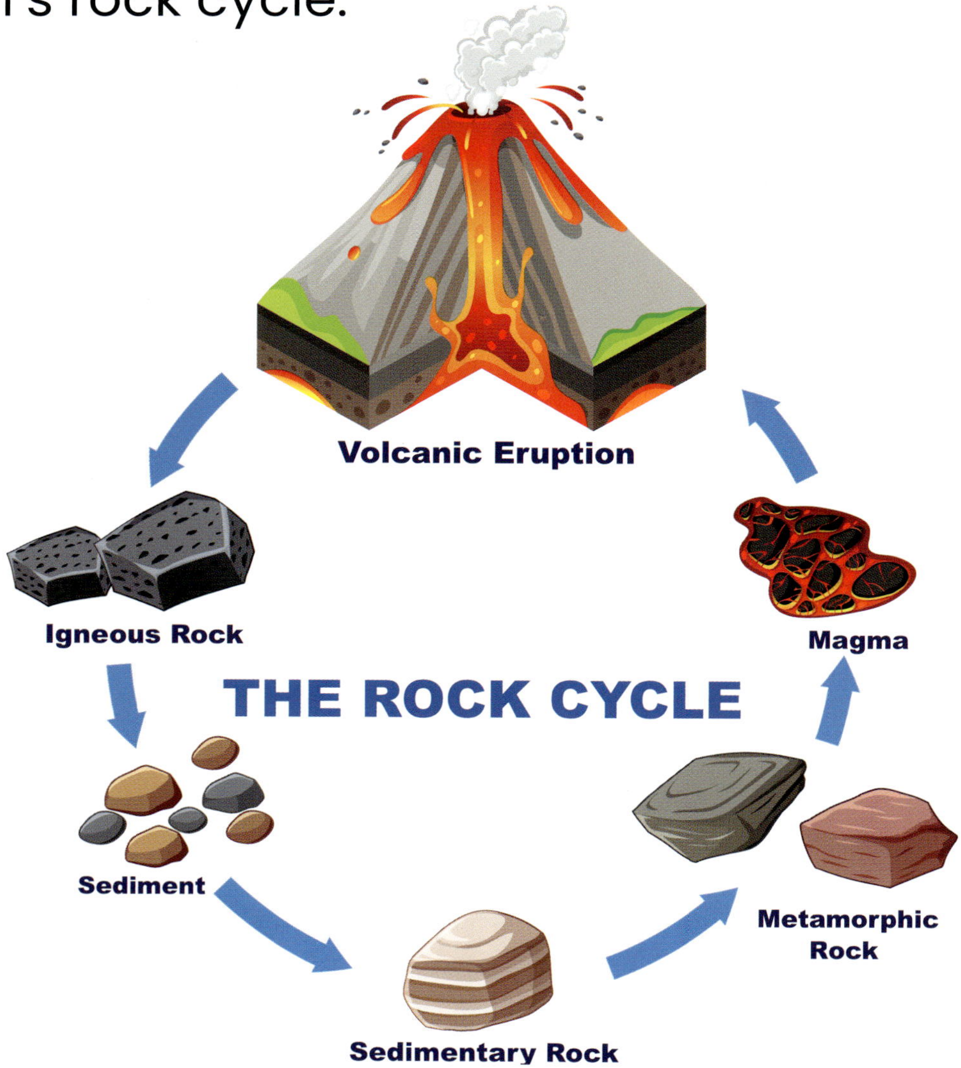

Most limestone begins in shallow ocean water. **Corals** live there along with clams and other shelled animals. When the creatures die, their skeletons or shells sink to the bottom.

Over time, lots of skeletons and shells pile up in layers. The layers of **sediment** get so heavy that everything in them is **compressed**. This **compaction** squishes minerals closer together.

Water flows around the layers. It carries minerals that act like glue. They make the layers stick together.

The minerals also harden the stuck-together layers. Over millions of years, the layers turn into rock.

WHERE IS LIMESTONE FOUND?

Limestone is found in places that were once covered by oceans. You can find limestone in parts of Germany, India, Japan, and many other countries.

The world's biggest limestone **quarry** is in Michigan in the United States. It has produced more than 700 million tons (635 million metric tons) of limestone since it opened more than 100 years ago.

Water that drips through limestone can **dissolve** the rock. Over time, it makes holes that can become caves.

Mammoth Cave is a series of limestone caves in Kentucky, U.S. It's the world's longest known cave system.

HOW IS LIMESTONE USED?

Limestone is easy to cut, so it's often used in buildings. It's also a main part of cement. Sidewalks, driveways, and roads may all have limestone in them.

Crushed limestone can be added to soil to help plants grow. It's also put in toothpaste to help scrub away bits of food.

Limestone is found around the world. This common rock is useful. People use it in buildings and much more. It even helps keep our teeth clean!

GLOSSARY

compaction (kuhm-PAK-shuhn): a process where small bits are pressed together over time so that the space between the pieces gets smaller

compressed (kuhm-PRESD): pressed together or flattened

corals (KOR-uhlz): tiny sea creatures whose skeletons join together to form coral reefs

dissolve (di-ZAHLV): to break down when mixed with water

fossils (FAH-suhlz): bones, shells, or other traces of animals and plants that lived millions of years ago

minerals (MIN-ur-uhlz): solids that form naturally in Earth and that do not come from an animal or plant; limestone contains minerals like calcite and dolomite

quarry (KWOR-ee): a place where rocks, sand, or minerals are dug out of the ground

sediment (SED-uh-muhnt): bits of natural materials, such as rocks or shells, that settle in layers

vinegar (VIN-i-gur): a sour liquid made from fermented juice

THINKING QUESTIONS

1. How are rocks put into groups?
2. Where is limestone found?
3. How do fossils help form limestone?
4. What is compaction?
5. Describe some of the ways people use limestone.

INDEX

ABOUT THE AUTHOR

Tracy Vonder Brink is always curious about the world around her. She loves to make facts and true stories fun and has written many books for kids. Tracy lives near Cincinnati, Ohio, and enjoys reading, hiking, and playing with her two rescue dogs.